true enough

*I ask for your love
and I have nothing to offer
but my own in return...*

~Diane Wakoski, *The Motorcycle Betrayal Poems*

true enough

poems of love and longing

by alan abrams

in memory

Carl Vogel
Linda Talbott
Cheryl Starke
Karen Thomas
Sheldon Abrams
Henrietta "Hank" Asen

dedicated to

Janet Deering Kinzer

Printed in the United States of America

ISBN 979-8-218-47312-9

First Edition

Cover photo by Jason Rylander

Sligo Creek Publishing Company
9039 Sligo Creek Parkway
Silver Spring, MD 20901
sligocreekpublishing.com

GratefullyAcknowledged

Autumn Sky Poetry Daily: "The Poetesses' Apartment"

Bourgeon: "To a Lover, Foolishly Abandoned," *"Aleinu,"*[1] "Limerence," "I Could Forgive Him"

El Portal: "Somewhere North of Ojo Sarco"

The Galway Review: "Reading Some Poetry on a Dreary Evening"

Knee Brace Press: "True Enough," "On Deck"

Neopoet Around the Globe: "Blood Brothers"

The Rat's Ass Review: "The Poet's Secrets"

The Raven's Perch: "Beatrice," "Her Fragrance"

Third Wednesday: "Learning to Cook"

---

[1] Nominated for the 2022 Pushcart Prize

Contents

The Poet's Secrets

With a sweet girl's love,
why be jealous of mere gods?
     ~Li Po

It's late, Li Po, but I've some questions,
as the moon rises behind a veil of mist,
shapely, yet demure: how did its silvery light
inspire your pen? And if I dare to ask—
how many lovers did your verses win you—
you've never written of their beauty or their charms.

And, who, please tell me, who
was your favorite? Did she ride you,
with her robe tied loosely round her pale plump belly
'til she blushed like the strawberry moon?
I beg you, Li Po, share your secrets with me.

The Poetesses' Apartment
For Anne Becker

To get there, you walk up a steep hill,
past the parking lot where the cars
are neither new nor luxurious. Then,
up some crumbling concrete steps,
to the entrance of a plain brick building—
and still two more flights inside,
 to the Poetesses' apartment. The hike

is well worth the effort,
because from its generous living room window
you can see the park, or at least its treetops.
The limited view may be an advantage,
because the rooftop of the next building
screens the parkway, where my ghost bikes
go blasting by—unbaffled Beemers, mostly,
but also a Norton ass shaker, a leaky Harley flathead,
and a one lung BSA. Other phantoms that inhabit
the environs include exes and old girlfriends. Also,
several places where you once could score a lid.

Inside, it's as though the Poetess has lived there
since an ounce cost ten bucks.
The thriving fern, the exhausted couch,
the dining room walls lined
with unfinished pine bookshelves;
the tabletop hidden by manuscripts.
The gray cat that sniffs in your direction
and leaves the room.

She apologizes for the mess,
but all the clutter fits perfectly,
like in a poem about a crazy love gone by.

Every Damn Thing
for Linda

The best love is crazy love. Crazy because it is true,
because truth is, all love is crazy. At least that's what I say,
and you would think, crazy as I am, that I would know.
I know you wanted my crazy love, maybe not so much
because it was true, but because it was truly crazy.
Every damn thing about it.

So what if it did not last. You moved on a lot sooner than I did.
I covered more territory, but you went further. I have no idea
how you loved your other lovers, but I'll bet they were all
crazy about you. Because I still am, in a crazy way,
even though you're gone. All this is true.
Every damn thing about it.

True Enough

...one can be in love with several people at the same time,
feel the same sorrow with each, and not betray any of them
~ Gabriel Garcia Marquez

Joe lost his old love to cancer. I don't say former, because he
still loved her, even though he has been with another for
many years now. There's nothing wrong about this—
many hearts are true enough to handle it. Her
dying happened in slow motion, like in a
dream you know is a dream but you
can't wake up from. You get to
an age when this shit is to be
expected; still it doesn't
diminish the pain.
Anyway, her
name was
Ruth

Her Fragrance

Was that a smile upon her lips,
that stranger I just passed—
who transfixed me with the rhythm of her hips—
does she look back?

Like as not, but what she leaves behind
is her scent—for me—alone—to find.

Thus I pass into her world,
where trace of rose and jasmine swirl,
and just for this sweet moment I possess her,
as surely as we lie, legs entwined,
til on the breeze her fragrance dissipates,
and I can no more hold her in my mind
than detain her in my arms.

At last I turn—too late—she is gone—
with all her aromatic charms.

Traces

When a warm, soft breeze filters
through the spruce, sighing,
for it knows it cannot linger,
I feel your gentle fingers on my shoulder.

And when dusky, slanting light
spills dappled shadows on the floor,
turning oak to gold, I see you dancing,
soundless, to the song of the setting sun.

And when the sickle moon
sweeps across the dawning sky,
harvesting the stars, I search among
the dewdrops for traces of you.

Playing with Fire

Did you ever play with matches
though your parents told you not to?
Of course you did, and so did I,
but did you scorch your brand new trousers,
or burn down the neighbor's shed? Or

when you turned sixteen, did you
clamber out your bedroom window,
and coast your father's car out of earshot?
Then where'd you drive, and who'd you meet?
And did you make it back before the dawn?

But what I really want to know
is if you ever kissed a woman
who you knew was someone's else's.
Did that kiss burn down their house or your own?
And are you happy now?

To a Redhead

Love is a fire that consumes common sense—
which it must, for lovers to unite; particularly
for you and I, who were so much alike
in our childish temperaments.

We made a lot of love at first;
it was that which kept us close.
But restless hearts breed jealousies,
and it finally came to blows.

Karen, I bear you no ill will,
these years we've been apart,
though when I found your brief obit,
you broke another piece of my battered heart.

Beatrice
You caged me in water…
~Diane Wakoski, *The Motorcycle Betrayal Poems*

Oh, my Beatrice!
you break like waves,
each one unique,
often criss-crossing,
and successive waves canceling
the retreat of the ones before.

Each crashing wave the same,
roaring cries of *love love love* —
each a different kind of love,
and each one I crave until
the next one breaks upon the sand.

Oh, my Beatrice!
I am tangled in the rigging
of the wreckage of my ship.
I am swept up by your current,
my fate is but your whim.
Where you will, I must go,
be it Paradise—or below

I Could Forgive Him

When the night talks to you, you gotta listen…
Look at that moon. Listen to that desert.
~from the movie *Electra Glide in Blue*

I was not made for abuse,
no, I was meant for a gentler hand
on my throttle, and a boot with
more finesse on my shifter.

But when I got to know him,
those sorrowful destinations
I took him to, those crazy friends
and troubled women he hung with,

I could forgive him. He needed
something to take his anger out on,
so it might as well have been me.
Truth be told, I got to enjoy it, like

that night he and Tony closed down
Mr Henry's. The headful of vodka
made him daring, dragging my
footpegs through the hairpin turns

of Beach Drive. Or when he held my
engine at redline, down the long hill
to the Wilson Bridge, his warm
belly tucked flat on my tank,

I couldn't help but give him all I had.
How proud we both were, when my
spedo needle froze at one hundred
and ten–I never knew I could go

so fast. But that night he met Ilene
I was so sure he was going to get
laid, until he blew the turn and
dumped her in the weeds. She

seemed like a nice girl, a good head
on her shoulders, who might have
done him some good. She wasn't
hurt, but my forks were bent. He

patched me up, dammit all, with second
hand parts that didn't match. Like
Ilene, it was too much for me to bear;
not long after, I threw a rod along

a lonely stretch of Route 66. Perhaps
a better man, with a warm garage
and a lighter touch, who loved
me for my classic lines, would

have kept me going. But I've ridden to
both coasts, and skirted the Gulf of Mexico,
blasted up dirt roads in the Rockies.
I've crossed blistering deserts, and

fired up at five below. Would I swap
all that for the nice garage, and
pleasant Sunday rides? No thank
you please, I'd rather rust away.

Limerence
For MAD

I followed you out west, when I was in despair;
you took me back, reluctantly. We spent the winter
in that tiny trailer house along a washboard road

where we spooned the frigid nights away—
then we'd wake to frosty halos on the wall,
where our heads had lain.

Though that infernal itch impelled me
to move on, I remember you most fondly,
when it went down to five below.

To a Lover, Foolishly Abandoned

What I wish for you: sunrise, with just the right
number of clouds, at just the right altitude,
to tint and refract slanting rays onto your garden;

air, mild and moist, a breeze strumming new leaves,
slipping through your open window like a stealthy
lover, gently waking you from slumber.

Coffee brewing aroma; a cat brushing your bare ankle;
chores, light and familiar that await you and no more.
Then, a walk to be taken, redbuds for color,

mock orange for fragrance, a lusty cardinal for a
merry song; redwing blackbirds, too, perched
on swaying cattails, calling for a mate.

Back home, books to be read, really,
too many of them, stacked on end table
and nightstand, one of them splayed

open on your chair, and maybe a story,
anxious to be told—just waiting for
evening's soothing silence and your pen.

Reading Some Poetry on a Dreary Evening
Michiko said, "The roses you gave me kept me awake
with the sound of the petals falling."
~Jack Gilbert, "Michiko Nogami (1946-1982)"

The poet's grieving
rises from these pages.
He mourns for his Michiko
perhaps even more
than for himself.

Out my window
only the nearest trees
can be seen through the mist.
Weather good for roses.

Elegy on a One-Nighter

Neither can the wave that has passed by be recalled,
nor the hour which has passed return again
        ~Ovid, *Ars Amatoria*

Up the slapdash steps, on the side of a small cape cod,
to your cozy little bedroom, that much closer to God.

Me with an introduction, and a jug of cheap red wine—
a little liquid something, to ensure the stars align,

and you with just a first name, and likewise me to you;
I drained the most of the jug, but you had plenty too,

before we tumbled into bed; me, benumbed enough to last
until I found your groove. Oh my what a blast

we had, losing our human selves, going completely wild;
and at the very end, how softly you smiled.

I climbed your stairs again to share another magic night,
but the spell was broken, and we could not get it right.

Now, as nights are more sedate, at time's infinite distance,
do I make too much of this, in memory's persistence?

No Crime

As if…those ice blue irises
along this faded picket fence
were deeded, and duly recorded
in florid script upon a yellowed page,
in some buckram bound folio
smelling of mold—*no*—
They were planted by a hand
long since departed;
they flourish in neglect,
and serve no greater purpose
than to entice a passing swain
to steal a handful for his sweetheart—
no crime there be, but
to let them grow in vain.

Cattle Call

I thought the girls were silly, back in nineteen sixty five, when they came out against the war, a million miles away.

Fast for peace, their buttons read, pinned to their swelling chests— feast for war! I mocked—they fired on us—let's blow them all away!

More intent was I on little Nancy Swope, when she shifted in her seat, and flashed a glimpse of pink between the buttons of her blouse.

But that day when class abruptly halted, and on the flickering screen, Lyndon Johnson came to life: My fellow Americans, he drawled, I need a hundred thousand more.

I swear I saw the words as they issued from his mouth, alive as they could be—I swear I knew right then and there that they were lies, they were lies.

A cattle call, David called it, when he returned from the war with some shit that blew us all away. A cattle call it was that caught him, back in nineteen sixty six.

Only three years later, I had a newborn daughter. I carried her one autumn night, among a million more, up Pennsylvania Avenue,

and placed a single candle on the wall, where another million candles cast their glow upon the White House lawn.

That baby kept me from the draft, after I quit school. Still, I envied those more brave, who burned their cards, and let the cops drag them away.

Not long after, David took my wife and child, and I drifted west; never was I bitter, though—I liked him anyway.

And now, by God! more than fifty years have passed; David's teeth are missing, lost to demons he brought home, that haunt him to this day.

Yes, I thought the girls were silly, though they were right— but even so, how did they know, how did they know?

We Had Sandy Point

In Dad's sky blue Bel Air,
bound for the Chesapeake shore,
the four of us on the front seat;
Mom's soft voice in song, keeping the beat
with cupped hand slapping her thigh;
my brother in her lap as farms flew by.

We passed by Mayo Beach, no dogs or Jews
read a sign beside its gate, not a new
sentiment to us. But sandy shore and salty waves
cared not to whom we prayed.
The Black folk had their Sparrow Beach,
and we had Sandy Point. To each

their own—as for us, our ice chest
filled with corned beef sandwiches, better yet,
pastrami, then slabs of chocolate cake.
But after eating Mom made us wait
an hour before dashing back into the tiny waves
that straggled up the Bay.

Exhausted, sun scorched, jellyfish stung,
we return to the car, in vain pursuit of setting sun.
I'd fall asleep in the back seat. Tomorrow
my back and arms would peel. Now
Mayo's sign is gone—so hatefully begotten—
though old prejudices be not forgotten.

On Roy Bentley's Grandmother's Attempt
To Shoot Her Lover

What of this gal, who had the wherewithal to rack a forty-five,
and the will to line up the sights on his forehead—
was she surprised, when the gun leapt at that first shot, or
did it bring back memories of her father, or some brother,
or maybe an earlier boyfriend standing behind her,
his arms enveloping her and steadying her own would-be lethal hands—
don't jerk it, squeeze it, BLAM! thatta girl...

Though they all knew she was crazy, it may be he had
it coming. But even so, how could she miss in nine tries?

And anyway, what lessons could she teach him,
by blowing out his brains?

Learning to Cook

Ridiculous, how many wives that I've run from—and
surrogate wives, and surrogate-surrogate wives, as
Cogs would say, speaking from his experience—and
who, it's worth mentioning, could drink circles around

me, and moreover, could hold his pee like the truck
that siphons out porta-potties. Cogs was not so much
interested in me as my old BMW, only marginally
badass, even with its unbaffled exhausts. He asked me

to take him for a ride, which I did, but I took it real
easy. For one thing, he was pretty bulky, and I'd already
had a few mishaps with a passenger on board. One,
which should have killed us both, and the other with

a woman named Ilene, who I was certain I was going
to bed with before I ran us off the road. Not to mention
that the bike didn't have much oomph, not even with one
rider, particularly compared to the crotch rockets of

recent years, with power an ordinary rider can only
dream of tapping. Furthermore, my permit had been
revoked. But Cogs was pleased enough to return the
favor, and took me for a screamer in his bathtub Porsche,

drifting all four wheels through sharp curves at redline,
me, bracing myself with my feet on the dash. Soon after, I
moved in with Cheryl. It breaks my heart to look at her
photo. Her only flaw was a ragged scar above her left knee

(see, I even remember which side), from when a truck ran
her into a ditch. She too rode a Beemer, but a late model
Slash Five, which I worked on at Cycle City. That's how
we met. Cheryl lived hard by the tracks, in an old

building clad with asbestos shingles. The freight trains
passing in the night were as soothing as my mother's
lullaby, I guess because we lived in Ivy City just after I
was born. You wouldn't think to look at me back then,

that I was seeking some sort of respectability, which is
why I invited Cogs to dinner. Steak, I thought, was the
way to go, but I bought chuck, being not only broke but
clueless about meat. I could have served my Red Wing

boots with as much success. Talk about clueless–
I knew even less about making good love than cooking
a good meal; that you can't get by on your meat alone.
What's more is that my own engine–like my bike–lacked

a lot of oomph. In the shame of failing to please her, I
drifted away. And from many others after her, before
I half-ass figured things out. Cheryl, who had by far the
nicest pair I'd ever beheld, died of breast cancer, proving

that even if there is a God, he is an SOB. Coughlin,
for all I know, is still careening around in the Porsche.
Me, like that lucky blind hog, finally found an acorn.
And I'm learning to be a decent cook.

Stuffed Cabbage
with a nod to Sid Gold

Grandma Mae told me Linda's butt was too big. As if.

And you know what she told her son
when he won admission to Brooklyn Tech?
You ain't gone to no tech school—
it's all the way across town—and anyway,
Mr. Hotshot—nobody's gonna hire a Jew,
even with an engineering degree.

But her stuffed cabbage was delicious—
meaty, salty, sweet with swollen raisins.
No wonder I loved her.

I could tell you more, how she bragged
that when she was little, during Christmastime,
she'd make a sling for her arm and hustle pennies
on Ocean Avenue. How that talent paid off,
making the most of worker's comp. Or when

she lost control of that Pontiac Chief,
went up the curb, drove half a block
down the sidewalk and merged back into traffic
without so much as a scratch.

I could tell you about that old cocker
someone fixed her up with after Grampa died.
How he liked sit around in his boxers watching wrestling.
It's not clear who threw who out, but we know
it was after she wrecked his Chrysler.

I could tell you more. Lots more.
But these are my treasures, not yours.
I'm sure you have your own.

Aleinu

Dear Allen Ginsberg, no angelheaded hipster am I,
nor have I ever seen those staggering Mohammedan angels–
not in my deepest swirling dreams. Some life force
always drew me back from the brink,
before plunging that angry needle in my arm.

But like you, Allen Ginsberg,
Jewish blood pulses in my veins, and
traces of Hebrew prayer linger in my brain.
Aleinu leshabeach la'adon hakol.
Our duty to praise. Yet I am a stranger
to the synagogue, and bare my head to the sun.

And I should tell you, Allen Ginsberg,
that I am straight, maybe with more authority
to say it than most men.
Because when I got in bed with Carl—
that night when we were nineteen, me,
with the scene flickering in my mind
of handsome Rupert Birkin and brawny Gerald Crich,
stripped naked, wrestling before the fireplace—
we, too, were naked, Carl and I, shoulder to shoulder,
hip to hip—but I could not get it up for him.
What was I thinking?

Sweet Carl, you were my dearest friend,
before you died of AIDS—still—
on our tentative night together,
I could not even touch your hard little cock.

But so what, Allen Ginsberg.
You still move me to tears,
Reading that poem about you and Jack
in that dead gray Frisco rail yard.
You showed me the golden sunflower
in the shadows of my tattered heart.
How I want to sing like you,
even in my own rusty voice.

Aleinu, our duty to praise.
Which is why I write this for you.

On Deck

We're on deck, Bob said,
when I told him about my mother—
how slow the step, how soft
the voice that once commanded
thirty sixth graders on the playground.
It was kind of him to ask.

I didn't know his folks, but I went with him
to mass when each one passed. Me,
I'm no longer frightened to look
into the eyes of an age-ravaged face. If I'm lucky,
it will be me who nurses Janet,
And not her, me. Batter Up!

Blood Brothers

My father knew his knots and splices, and
how to wind a hose in even loops without a kink.
These were skills he learned in boot camp, before
shipping out across the often lethal seas. Later,
with a house, a car, two kids, and a dreamboat
wife, Saturdays would find him on the roof, painting
the hatch with red lead, or out front, rotating the tires

of the turquoise Bel Air, teaching me the criss-cross
pattern. I was soon condemned to tend the lawn, with
that infernal push-reel mower; while mom, squatting
on her bare show-girl legs, pried out crabgrass with a
fork bladed tool. After chores, Frankie and I dared
each other to leap into the basement well, where just
below the edge hung the hose, coiled on its rack. An

errant loop caught my foot in mid air, slamming my
forehead against the edge of the concrete step beyond.
Frankie cried he's dying, as blood drenched my
face. Mom dashed out the kitchen door, and met me
halfway up the wooden steps. Dad right behind her,
with her best tea towel, to staunch the flow. Then,
off to Dr. Lachman, who met us in his walk-up office,

to get the gash stitched up. Dad had seen his share
of blood, men in boats blasted apart, and the maimed
and wounded his ship ferried back from Normandy.
He mortified a German prisoner, hooked to an IV,
telling him the fluid that trickled into his arm was
Juden's blut. Then he showed the man his dog tag, that
labeled him as Hebrew. How he loved to tell that story!

Now we both had scars–his, a whitish almond shape imprinted on his buttock–from playing football in a vacant lot strewn with broken glass. Afraid of what his mom would say, he asked the pharmacist to sew it up. And me, proud of the bandage over my eye. We made a brotherhood of blood. The scar lingers, a slanting crease among the horizontal furrows, plowed by time across my brow.

Oh, the Water

On the way back home we sang a song
But our throats were getting dry
  ~Van Morrison

Her hand slowly rises from the sheet. Its back
traced with thin meandering lines, red and blue—
a road map, perhaps, to a place she'd rather be.
A bony finger points to a glass of water. The straw

placed between ashen lips; she takes
a tiny sip, coughs a gurgling cough—which,
says the nurse, could induce pneumonia—
and that would be the end. But for now

we hold hands, gaze at photographs of her honeymoon
in the Catskills. Beside a manicured pond, she rocks
a two piece bathing suit; he kid-grins in skimpy trunks,
shy-proud of a handsome body just beginning to get soft.
A boy who learned to swim in Sheepshead Bay,
he joined the Navy on the day he turned 18.The LST
he served on launched first wave troops
to Omaha Beach, then retrieved their mangled bodies
from its bloody waters. Survival made him headstrong—
even more than as a cocky youth. Spotted her across
the dance floor, had to have his way. But by the time
two kids arrived, MS sunk their dreams. She became

a teacher, barely kept her family afloat. Fed
and bathed her husband, too, flushed his bladder
with saline solution—yet another mournful
memory of the sea. Somehow she kept her looks,
buried two more after him.More water,

she mumbles, in a feeble voice that once commanded
thirty rowdy children, that once long ago sang a lullaby
to me. Again the straw held up to her mouth, while
salty tears trickle down my grizzled cheeks.

Stone on Stone

"Caw caw caw crows shriek in the
white sun over the grave stones... "
    ~Allen Ginsberg, "Kaddish"

Headlights lit in the middle of the day
we follow the man (who I'd now call young)
borne in heavy traffic through the heart
of town to a district of deceptive winding roads
and project housing with trampled lawns,
shattered bottles, and enumerable crows
that ignore the iron gates guarding
a deep narrow lot.
              There, a phalanx
of dull grey stones,
some leaning this way and that, and all
advancing toward a chapel of yellow brick.
This is our destination.
              He'd said
to me, not long before
I want to die, knowing full well I agreed,
suffering as he did, and for so long.
                    I still
get lost whenever I return
to snatch up a chunk of gravel
from where we park, to place it
in remembrance on his stone.

Stone on stone, over the bones
of the man I called my father.

All of This Is True

A classic exit affair, she called it—
and the diploma on the wall
backed up her assertion.
I've seen enough of this,
she said, to warn you that
the odds aren't in your favor.

But even when they're stolen,
the seeds of love will flourish
if they fall on fertile soil,
and passions well tended
bring forth the bounty of devotion.
Nineteen years proves all of this is true.